MEDIATED

MEDIATED

Carol Mirakove

FACTORY SCHOOL
2006

Acknowledgments

I extend grateful acknowledgement to the facilitators of the public spaces in which some of these poems first appeared: Mónica de la Torre and Tonya Foster, Segue Reading Series; Laura Elrick and Rodrigo Toscano, *Capilano Review*; Frank Sherlock, Night Flag Reading Series; Brendan Lorber, Zinc Bar Talk-Reading Series; Aaron Levy, Slought Networks; Erik Sweet, *Tool: A Magazine*; Hannah Sassaman, *Xconnect*; Kaia Sand and Jules Boykoff, TangentRadio; Greg Fuchs, FEVA radio; Allison Cobb, Jennifer Coleman, Ethan Fugate, Susan Landers, *Pom2*; Bruce Andrews, *New Yipes Reader*; Jena Osman, Juliana Spahr, and Gary Sullivan, *Chain*; Susana Gardner, *Dusie*; Elizabeth Treadwell, *Outlet*; Sam Ladkin and Robin Purves, *Edinburgh Review;* Mark Nowak, *XCP*. Core thanks to Allison Cobb, Pattie McCarthy, Jenn McCreary, Katie Mugnai, and Janice Tumulty for life support; to Steve Carll for outreach; and to Bill Marsh for his inventive and generous editorship. – CM

Cover image: Carol Mirakove
Production Assistants: Octavia Davis, J.R. Osborn

Mediated, Carol Mirakove
First Edition, Factory School 2006
Heretical Texts: Volume 2, Number 5
Series Editor: Bill Marsh

ISBN 1-60001-049-0

factoryschool.org

CONTENTS

MEDIATED   7

FUCK THE POLIS

traffic was hectic   31
drop your weapons.   33
& then there's the cute story about Nancy Reagan
         freshening her make-up during the drug bust   34
police (the case) (es)   36
sasha the kid assassin   39
hostile takeover takeover   40
CRASH stands for Community Resources
         Against Street Hoodlums   42
the polis   45

PROPAGANDA

IT HAS GOTTEN HARD   51
WE NEED TO TALK   52
I'M TRYING TO DECIDE WHO TO VOTE FOR   53
I'M KEEPING ON   54
THIS MORNING TERMINATION   55
THE WEALTH IN YOU   56
I SAW HOUSES OF WATER   57
TIMES OF THE PEOPLE   58
THERE WAS A NOTE   59
OUT OF WHERE YOU ARE NOT   60
EVEN IN LAB COATS   61
COUNTER CULT   62
THE LINE BEYOND WORK   63
WAR IS AT PLANET   64
WAIT.   65

PORNOGRAPHY

boy on fence   69
"closely-related process of differentiation..."   70
congruence   71
positions   72
barely legal   74
windows are handled   75
cow and tree   76
girl in dunes   77
roll credits   78
I like babies born & raised   79
"you claim to be clean, yet you reject your own taste"   80
human traffic   81
blind fold   83
my frame my chain of sugars I felt
        like status being inside   84
do you want someone to keep you honest?   85
warden situ   86
extensity   87
bending veil   88
mind the empty [vile]   89
morning glory   90

COMMUNITY THANKS

COMMUNITY THANKS   91

————MEDIATED————

<Subject> awake   awake   psychographic? <End of Message>

Headline: "No Matter How Much Energy We Conserve, We're Still Going to Need More Energy" — President Bush, May 18, 2001 *(Continued)*

Headline: US Warns Hugo Chavez Labeled OPEC Lunatic *(Continued)*

<Subject> rock smash scissors <End of Message>

Headline: Prosecutor in Coup Case Assassinated *(Continued)*

Headline: Poppy Crop Fire Scare Again Tops Economic Charts *(Continued)*

<Subject> makes a bedspread & is so taken by the colors & patterns of the bedspread she only vaguely sees the other objects in the room — she only sees a fragment of the whole. this happens because she is, we are, conditioned to — and have deep biological needs towards — pleasure. <End of Message>

Headline: NAFTA, CAFTA, & the Poverty After *(Continued)*

Headline: Lula Dubbed Cardoso II, May Yet Have Tricks Up Sleeve [One Hopes] *(Continued)*

<Subject> in my bed we are sleeping in the dreaming/nightmare beds we make <End of Message>

Headline: Boom Hum Factors Mexico's Border, Crosses Disillusioned *(Continued)*

Headline: Four Waltons Co-Appointed Secretary of Starvation *(Continued)*

<Subject> last night I dreamt I made a pillowcase in the presence of an old man who sold bed sheets. outside there were kids playing jumping off stumps <End of Message>

Headline: "We're Losing" — Colin Powell, January 12, 2005 *(Continued)*

<Subject> aperture, that smell, endooring <End of Message>

Headline: Bolivia fights back! *(Continued)*

<Subject> gets on the Q train, hears a woman talking to her sons who are near 8 years old. she is talking about people dying in war, saying "This is why you have to go around the world and meet people; so we can learn to get along, and we don't have all this fighting." she says "One person can make a difference. You can." and one of the boys says, "Do you make a difference?" and she says, "I try. For example, have you -ever- heard me say that I hate anyone? Have I ever in your whole lives spanked you? Do I scream at you?" <End of Message>

Headline: Mercosur Maquiladora China Building Dwelling Think *(Continued)*

<Subject> with you while apart <End of Mess

      between
files & a click
down we are in
the fragile grip, deal.
      controversy & they nerve
to say wet we are not
& among them.

animals
disposable brute fact of contingency
burns them away like slag   spit hips &
rooftop
                glimmers, commitments
                        of angels (ours) falling
                from & sky, go

                                                falling
                                        from & sky, go

you a walking forest   me with city smoke

it makes little sense to not be complex, muting in an ear
leaves chained an archived document to
affront
shellac   she is susceptible to faith.

                    inch Allah   [stop] gap that god
          matters
what you are – found – collective
                              scale-jumping passion
in discovery
from chaos
          factories?   labor doesn't live here anymore
                    float
                    problem   the eliminal   human

                              Cassandra the future
                              she'd wake up
                              a core dump
                              departure does this work?

                              for you?

                              you must choose?

                              sides? apparently you break

               "or do something else"

                                        & yet determined
          side   not side   she is let go to one the pledge

                    How do   they   present
                         a   "glass house"
                    to their   constituencies?

                    about face.

12

something with someone specific but not certain.
switching back the guttered ballerina and the sun
/ spoked / parking / structure / pretty & delirious.
weeds bend the boredom dandelioned.

I want
to be   a dandelion.

so not, "They were in love. Fuck the war."
but "They were in love and they would level the war
                                        mongers."

> *My friend the poet CAConrad told me that*
> *dandelions normalize blood-sugar levels*
> *& asks me if I've noticed that lawns in this*
> *country are filled with them. I say yes & he*
> *thinks the plants are telling us we eat too*
> *much sugar. I wonder & I wonder too if*
> *they are ubiquitous because by putting so*
> *much sugar in our soil through our waste the*
> *dandelions pop to balance the ground.*
>
> *& I want to say, forgive my naïveté (forgive?)*
> *– because it isn't – willful(?)*

I finally understood the concretians when I read an analysis of an
esteemed architect by which the architect had allegedly designed
his arches in Ls because "El" is a word for God and he was
allegedly putting, or looking, for God everywhere, I was, or it was,
conversation & in too fragile to suggest, the notion of best practices
in structural engineering, cheap materials, endurance.

[ticker] billboard aura, anybone, we are the you in future. a rush at
the bar looks justified. does he have a pet, or a bed, I couldn't hear?
[ticker] the pulls while kids twirl flutes & louts before a fireplace,
eyes, rolled back not out – so as to stand a presence.

let's get abducted. car seat in the woods, rock horse in the desert
& some tumble. is there noise? yes there is big noise and mind you
even bigger ears. we tall & tangent shadows.

there are five of them & form a rhombus little constellation. & we go
with "them," we go with any "them"s, with all the time in the world.

let's have all the time in the world.

& not worry that that makes no sense our blazen melee
megaphones. & not worry that all the time in the world might be, in
fact, ecologically brief.

not worry

silver. paint. Mars? here. pay attention.
                                                &

            "don't wake the architect"
"it's really hard to see"
                    "all right I'll be quiet"
            "careful" –

                            the clearing air could be a lie.
                            the man who told me that a heart
                            is a picture of a woman bending
                            over broke mine in that
                                                            facing
                                            up

                    "for love I would" it's really not that

                    hard?

                    to see?

I am learning a hard lesson from these class discussions.
I want to say I am consistent but I misspell consistant. ant.
I answer the survey on reactions to cross-species gene-
expressions. I can make myself convincing monkeys elves
& aliens. which is the tremendous success of gauge theory,
located in that it can be located, isolated, virtually benign.

is it arrogant of science
to appropriate QED as
an acronym for quantum
electrodynamics? or should
we be happy to think on
abbreviations as related.

my friend Rob says appropriation just -is- and he is right
that is not wrong.

I tend a rosary inflated.

erratic terrain is it or am I

your veil
through which I see
a hairline
adolescent
adoration
of your context
dropout [bang bang]
concrete
concrete daybook

burning   listed books
to guard   enlisted books
now out of school
I found the boy
impelled by sky by
nursing very pressing
on my chest   & protein
settles
on my farm.
Claude and Clara
settle on my farm.
I hear soil, understand,
& what I hear him mean
[the dead]
when he says
("him")
he says
"I meet with
these people all the time.
I know how they think.

I meet
with them all the time.
I meet with
Sylvio
Berlus[syllables]…"

syllables are what
I understand
when they
when they
when they they
other me.

pay attention   it's free

"most things at school worry me"

the girl was set loose altogether

the boy had been bronzed
himself among the photographer.
the old trick of the caliber.
every step he made he was watched. or believed as much.
his restless-dream library wakes up blind saying
"love" without a human target. so as to not miss.
everyone else in the militant, debutante, seriously, time?

I don't
understand
how money
works
its reference
        points our
                units   meaning
                sex   recycle

        & about

                        face

        value:

                        you didn't
                        have
                        to say
                        a word.

hi!
hi.
hi!
car!
car!
more?
more.
is that pooh?
pooh!
good night.
night night.

+

Wife at bar: Joe, will you stop being [shakes her head] [shakes her head] whoever you are?
Joe: I gotta go to OTB.
Wife: OK.

+

woman in parking lot: I'm thinking about having my Social Security check direct-deposited to Wal-Mart.

+

Alex, the database administrator: We'll burn that bridge when we get to it.

+

Marketer, to subject of focus group: Do you feel lonely when you eat white bread?
Subject: Do I feel *lonely*?
Marketer: Yes, do you feel lonely when you eat white bread?
Subject: A little.

           sponge monkey   barren coated
clamps a throat   takes
                a splint
                        sucktank
                abducted weapon
                        at the stucco
                                rave
                        lick the brut
                triumvirate: racket
                        spice limb
— limber —   [ticker]   pull
        production imports
metal America
powerlines
a spotlight   autobody
        [Euro]body
    boxed up
                coldcut
    graffiti ripe
brickstained & magnetic

autobody   [€]body
                boxed up   SHOP
        my bloody hands
        your broken fist   a penny auction

                                        QUIT.

                    to see that seeing
                    is believing, sees believing is believing
                    too
                              a child moist will burst erasure
                              barely grounded sprouts with wonder
                                                          footing
                    — transfer —
     wonders dizzy
     & less dangerous
                    than criteria
                    sets interpretation like a trap
                    — sort —

        about face

        weather :: confession

on family, asylum, that is blacked out in blocking,
filters, subconscious erected, the author suggestion.
what is the range of the normal-neurotic and why not manage
both?

she knew it well, my litmus for quality, linked to
the pelvis, soul / delicious / quotient / wretched creatured
to a sway.

exit stage there is no stage.

last night I dreamt there were small clam shells all around the
perimeter of my bed. I seemed to be sure that when clams are
lured to your bed, it means that you are dirty. worse, the clams had
escaped and were on the loose. I thought to try and save them back
to sea, but realized that they must have died in seconds.

hidden repercussion rolls in bed & captures house
in blankets, fingers, & her mouth in stealing you
abreast & bundled

channels her inner black cat

through the drinking glass

                    monumental crisis commune
          kamikazee resist but the panic reaction
starting point it n e v e r   m e n t i o n s   c a p i t a l
cosmic knots relentless fuel vampiric penchants, ribbon
cut the wars on TV runnning through the tiled halls,
fast from her guilt cops micro-
political over-
heard to give herself
to others, that holds true,
in under-
adoration
calm

they are almost home when they fall dormant. triangle bermuda far
from slowing down slow down these lives depend on
                                        sshhh —

I meet my meetings did not know the boy.
herself. talk to him. not an audience of which he is a
part. she said. "why waste a bomb?"

[stick figure with gun]

      neither done nor gone I can feel   (the sun)
like I'm speaking white subtitles
on a bleached-out film
      strip "plastic poetry"
they sing
"que sera, sera"
& in a store
front they
paint "© yourself"
an icon in the laminate
suicide
      to feign
      in balance warped
      & feel like
         a liar put
      a place
      in place

a synapse
      extinguished & cheered
         a santé
./smack.sh
a face she
      comes at a
      cost & they are coming :
         disembodied in parades
      were to perish
in and in
      an underestimation
      of what I might love

      "we are the cause of hunger"

your mouth is right & pins
down my uncertainty

for pain in the world
for joy in the world
for currents we channel

anguish
desires
a causal body

with one hand on your back
and another in a tunnel

passing through invoked
caverns & conscious
                faults
        inadequately humbled
        taken
        to freefall
                & firmly
        abandon
in the forcefully captured
present, precisely
        to view | history
                        the bondage of karma
                        the dripping
branches
breaking
        out of the carriage &
                                looking
                                        up
        tensegrity
                tangled we might be
sin:
we live without.
shooting
in a bigbad
babybird
sky

*Where is
the remote?*

control?

[Latin American history is laundered in dead heroes]

Torrijos for the Canal
& Roldos for petroleum
& Allende for communism
& Sandinistas for health care, nutrition, for "the threat of a good
        example"
& Arbenz for land reform, United Fruit
& Goulard for wealth redistribution
& Chavez for the oil
& Bolivia for the water

Bolivia fought back
Venezuela fought back

they won we could be
winning

[January 20, 2005]

Washington, DC:

Q: "What do you think was the message of the inauguration?"
A: "Ownership society for everybody!"

                         freedom / for / your / freedom !

◘ Heard on Democracy Now!, January 21, 2005. The question was asked by Amy Goodman; the answer was provided by Vivian, a native Cuban, who now "owns a piece of America."

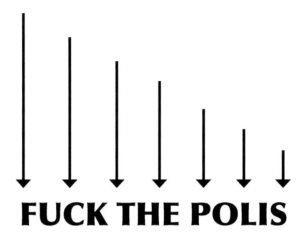

FUCK THE POLIS

Los Angeles, California: 1999–2001

Disremembered and unaccounted for, she cannot be lost because no one is looking for her.
— Toni Morrison, *Beloved*

traffic was hectic

I fucking panic in nature, even at pictures of it. but if everyone could
stop giving their jobs overtime,
            even if they didn't know why they had to,
necessarily

armchair genius over phattus apparatus:
site beat down into bankruptcy, consequent to
"invisible hours" in the workforce
                            a sort of free-
                reigning entity, as most portals have us
                                            believe.
I could sign up as a 'human' editor,
or whatever you call
                the non-paid kind & sleep
        the earthquake

I have a view of the man-made silver lake
which is pretty / from high up it
changes color like a mood ring or maybe
the middle of the LA river.
I do remember
having the same reaction to it as I did his 40-foot-
translucent brain as data-chopped suey.
it would seem I'd be healthier for getting used
                to flake culture:
                quotidian take compartmentalized
        into rock-star groupies getting romper
room on purpose, pale & congested, saying 'yes' all the time
is dangerous, & frankly, it bores   you resume
        & a mouthful of praise a little sick
                but refusing to check in

he looks all tan-and-away:
there must be more general goals. when our local social demands,
shopping can boost
energy levels without the negative side effects of coffee or of meth.
(except that's a myth.)

getting off the freeway I see a supermarket cart tied to a post in
yellow police tape reading ARE YOU UNBREAKABLE.COM
I think, how unlikely to find guerilla art in north hollywood. &
I'm thinking it's powerful: online 'living' + prepackaged chemical
consumerism, breaking us. but later jacking in I find that www.
areyouunbreakable.com is the url of a new blockbuster movie.

"Everybody knew what she was called, but nobody anywhere knew
her name."

then there was the guy on olympic blvd in west LA ardently
photographing the billboard of the airbrushed siren, or goddess, or
symbol of the fit
population

drop your weapons.

luminescent chains what the mourning sun incinerates the strata
to the south — "this is one low-ass ceiling." I just / don't trust 'em /
flesh / accident / shake-on-it eastside eastside up eastside

downtown there are 28,000 "garment" (sweatshop) workers.

to kiss it each & deem it naked. print & faint the quotations. out of
context, the "should be reproduceable by anyone" fantasy. what
about the city fires? I know the buildings but who
was in them.

hallucination pines & allow me to couch: these replies with pangs
of "freedom."

an aside: why one is not very useful. a smoke-filled alley as it
regrets, being hidden, remaining, "since we suffer" /
the privilege   being borne   into a race

centered ears window up winding tramps & so it would come down
to quantitative? couldn't the equation work, conversely? I mean,
isn't that a Kantian ethic? I mean, minus the class. a gross question.
issues that when I hear "remnant," I think, what luxury. cut up as
such. to sit in an evening
                                        dictee
                    "my teeth"

bitter intersection surplus take me too, trans-shock & imagine to
flora. there are right ways to make room for sleep yet I mailed you
not one & thus I am mortified. the whole it smacks, extinguish to
revisit

& then there's that cute story about Nancy Reagan freshening her make-up during the drug bust

April 6, 1989: [Nancy Reagan], accompanied by [Los Angeles Police] Chief [Daryl] Gates and a small army of Secret Service agents, toured the enemy fortress with its occupants still bound on the floor in flabbergasted submission. After frowning at the tawdry wallpaper and drug-bust debris, Nancy, who looked fetching in her LAPD windbreaker, managed to delve instantly into the dark hearts at her feet and declare: "These people here are beyond the point of teaching and rehabilitating."

— Mike Davis, *City of Quartz*

shipped the propaganda factory, fifty to a fishbowl & complaints heard in the hallway that "even though they're plastic, you still gotta feed 'em."

is this what white people mean by "hugs"?

Nancy & astronomy: preside the judgment hour & prescribe a yesterday, the future

claws approval polls polluted — call it racial riot. blown-away fanatics crack the seal of disapproval. little fish, face down, scrapes the broken sidewalk.

ask the CIA, on polygraph, how the drug-spikes occurred. out-of-reach / most likely / at-large / could explain the epidemic.

another yet-to-be-realized earth-day victory, curtained for the profit lies.

begins at conception. ends at birth.

witchery for global warning: what that could mean when out of
context. the chlorine campaign yields & more disease. endless in its
champagne manicure. still ruling — frozen bodies

arrested in collegial hangings. drudge report the following
questions: grips the accidental deaths too under lock & key.

+

humility of the history apart from the historical. ground. a severe
incubation. concrete / off ramp. last in line / historicity thud

on a limb could history? their dead spoken present record. as fish
pour, as fish eaten by

'education' / unsustained

red from awkward. ground from askew. green from shhh. lacking a
precedence a gesture splats gold after swept under. she: anonyme a
toe-tag the blunt — recall — the final space is every space, gripping

ambivalent pictures or the blank in the fluid swallows reading and
now. in the ground. at her shoes. gold. from the gone-ugly green: or
gold.

parsing out conglomerates of ambivalence & labeled. dumb /
without means. the awkward target whose harsh stab now grounds.
now molding. chokes.

[SWAT stands for Special Weapons and Tactics]

police (the case) (es)

Compton police department is disbanded: September 16, 2000

following, shouting, the city a loud balance. there are basic
problems. not all statements are protected, public / employee.
mayor is necessary leveling and expert, to consult an advance
before they actually talk / we are trying / to serve forward as a matter
of impose chilling. dead dogs. graduate of. "looking back it was [/]
positive."

"I think"   "I think"   the redevelopment the police union
voted no confidence & "I think" prides himself on 100 million
dollars. of infrastructure.

to dismantle, he shrugs off, he will win. "I don't see.. a problem,"
Bradley said. filmic.

compton scattering :: the cure

...four officers filed a civil rights lawsuit against the city government
in September, [citing that Compton Mayor Omar] Bradley sought to
dismantle the department to silence his critics.
— Online Forty Niner

the wavelength does not change.

light with energy for such a collision — that punctuation / should be
haphazard?

delta = delta the subzero power & indeed the mass electron.
one minus — no more the cosign. x-rays demonstrate [figure the
incident] comparatively

The decision sparked protests and marches throughout Compton. Lorraine Cervantes, 59, a local activist, says Mayor Omar Bradley should have put the decision to a citywide vote. "We're living in a democracy, aren't we?"

— USAToday

how science doubles back on itself: if imposed order of the LAPD, then entropy in Compton. must freedom, exclusively, yield chaos? & isolated.

Gary of Venice Beach writes:

I visited the cemetery to put flowers on my little brother's grave. It is overrun by gophers. It appears to be a serious health hazard for visitors.

frost / easy / don't / move

standard molar entropy

According to the Second Law of Thermodynamics, isolated systems tend to proceed toward higher entropy.

we use to symbolize: the degree, that particles more cluttered progress soars. "I place papers in [ ] cabinets. in other words, I upset"   "from the outside"

"solutions have a greater entropy than "

"do you know which way the jail is?" I don't. my car is broken.

the municipality.. spent 70% of its budget on 'public safety'. The police force of Compton, which [was] financed through this money, [had] gained a reputation as bad as the one of the LAPD.

— Eric Wright on Compton City

but it wasn't, then, the LAPD. or the feds, for that matter. better?
blood of the flash game. a clear loser, lacking industry / enter /
hip hop rap top hypercomp / defiance. (gangsters are, ultimately,
obedient.) (this is not a criticism: it is however obvious & very,
unapologetically, an unmediated marginalization.)

the reality strategy aims to home the horror. who are these tireless
confidence boosters. males reside paradoxically & hook the sad
sequence. based in. look at the shot patterns. a regular west-coast
spraying.

new generation brings more gangs

USA Today reports that Crips and Bloods are on tape laughing. who
knows why. seems it's a violation across the board. (it's called a '40,'
by the way.)

"murders"   "compared with"   "during the same time" "gang-
related"   "enjoyed a steady decline":   number dropped.
plummeted. under the plan. during "would save lives and [/] 7
million [dollars] a year."

& so he outspent. there will be children to track, the tally of a bingo:
didn't want / dizzying the ballot count didn't merely catch. on. own
people the most but worn, a real shot & the fete :: happy. formerly
of, time and a half. hatted, & complicit provides the arrangement, &
bows.

they were the young americans.

sasha the kid assassin

not a lot of vegetable matter.

I had a nightmare & a fascist, whose favorite pasttime is discrediting my intelligence. as we've said, we're not the chefs. it makes sense that you cld jump right on it. I don't know, I insist & I bail on the pre-bridal base text.

like what you say abt a subtext-free life as the goal. then I thought, "hey! what's taking you fuckers so long to call us?!"

gracious.

I get the vibe that this place is a money-centric mess of an outfit. "I am happiest and most effective when part of a dedicated and ambitious team."

the SoCal Library of Social Research? she'd sooner expect the moon to cheese. he bought me two copies of the book I left on your chair when he thought he was buying two different books. by the time I was crushed I didn't necessarily want to be heard, actually. cf. d2kla.org.

and yet he's not an addict. he yells at the tv kids when those anti-cigarette ads come on: oh, go ahead & smoke, you might as well! rhythm_bitch, delinquents.

the dead?

words?

hostile takeover takeover

it was [ad infinitum] the confrontation that led to silence

[In June 2000] Mayor Omar Bradley of Compton petitioned Cardinal Mahoney to order Father Stan Bosch to stay away from all future city council meetings. ..Father Bosch [had begun] taking members of his parish to city council meetings to protest a council proposal to disband the Compton city police department.. simply to ask for some accountability in terms of what is happening in the city.
— Los Angeles Lay Catholic Mission

staving off violence or trying over Father Stan. the new "less than honorable": metal detectors. "was there any actual violence?" "No,"

& possible place, basically would prevent uprising, decided, we could at least contain. presuppose destructive forces. might be within an organized next. "I can't say the names,"

"I don't know the names,
we started to ask the 'why' questions —

there are persons sometimes paid. sometimes encouraged. those kinds. strictly to try. elicit / illicit. "agitators." "well because" [as reported]   I trust / issued.

"I don't know the names,"

On Tuesday, July 9, city police set up special barricades around the council chambers after all 160 seats in the chambers had been filled. Outside, protesters waved copies of a city law that requires all council proceedings to be open to everyone.
— Los Angeles Lay Catholic Mission

influx of immigrants (or, ", a very essential connection among ourselves.")

from our day-to-day life. one degenerate politician "that's all I can afford." blatantly identified — the aberration to deter. peace to this resilient — community — purchase translation & propel the instrumental, vis-a-vis narcotics.

forward in the transition: homelessness. federal and state / grants to the city, already committed, a done / deal.

dead, dogs, black, sabbath. sunday, bloody but "was there any actual violence? No,

confirmed. lateral? linear.

the dead?

strained relations: remedy what might have been. noise. much? motivation, indicated that. "the city prevailed. And of course nothing

"But that's what"

"that's what.. peaceful intention was"

the voters   know how to forgive.

the hell we do.

CRASH stands for Community Resources Against Street Hoodlums

Dear Keston,

the Feds took over the LAPD three days after the LAPD took over Compton's police department. I can't help but smell a sinister motivation in the timing — the LAPD was witnessing the increasing leaks of its own crimes. falling from its historical glory (it had received praise akin to that which NY Mayor Giuliani now receives, i.e., "I don't care how he does it, the city is safer now"). would the LAPD assume control of Compton's force, whereby they'd (1) become larger and get more city funding, and (2) establish a reputation of achieving remarkable "results," in order to distract from the corruption of their internal affairs? I find it baffling.

meanwhile, the mayor and city council were eager to pawn off the Compton PD (plenty corrupt itself) because their constituents were screaming about crime. handoff to the LAPD meant that crime was no longer an issue for Compton's officials. election is a warm gun, etc.

Dear Elizabeth,

I suspect that Compton was set up / to be used / as a "playground" of sorts for the tough boys to revive the militaristic reputation they enjoyed throughout the 80s, so that they might thwart the probings into their scandal-laden cells.

I'm also reading a weird book from the 1950s on Christian-based leisure.

Dear Citizen,

while the actual takeover was processed too late for it to have been of any possible use to the LAPD, it is my contention that this commingling would seem, necessarily, to have been long in the making.

as it affects Los Angeles proper, media on the after-the-fact Rampart scandals are voluminous.

3.18.97
white cop shoots & kills off-duty black cop, says, "In my training experience this guy had 'I'm a gang member' written all over him."

11.6.97
Bank of America is taken for $722,000 & officer David Mack is implicated in the heist.

2.26.98
LAPD officer Brian Hewitt, of the Rampart division's prestigious anti-gang unit, CRASH, beats gang member Ismael Jimenez until he vomits blood.

3.27.98
Six pounds of cocaine is declared missing from the LAPD property room.

Make that seven.

5.98
Rampart Corruption Task Force is appointed, focuses on Officer Rafael Perez.

9.8.99
Perez comes to name 70 Rampart-CRASH officers as being wrapped in illegal happenings.

9.16.99
100 quote-unquote criminal convictions are overturned.

3.3.00
CRASH is disbanded.

9.19.00
The U.S. Department of Justice is set to monitor LAPD reforms over a five-year period.

11.21.00
The Rampart story ends in record settlements, costing the city $125 million.

the polis

:: attested

that the polis would develop in consequence of colonization, that
splitting, central to the concept. losing its autonomy would not
— neighbor — the splitting in the archaic period.

*she says. "I'm bad and I'm going to hell, and I don't care. I'd rather
be in hell than anywhere where you are."*

kitten. lapse. milk. saucer. in the shower

"conurbation (walled or unwalled) and whenever"

religion versus polis. religion versus a sense of town. religion
versus aesthetic. religion versus anti-religion. religion versus free
to be. religion versus greed what a hoot. there are so many ways
in which to be greedy / versus adequate, which is to say effective
rendering

once, I read an article about African mathematicians having
established fractal patterns in the construction of their villages.
but they weren't very quick to publish, & no sale, then, it goes / to
Europe / another / dommage.

such a map that would reveal

"because you are"   "despite your name"

"what time is it"   "I'll slap" [you]

ok "this [isn't] Easter" —

marginalia: *Faulkner* [for example] *doesn't allow Dilsey to discover
the consciousness we want / to see.*

he loaded himself monotonously: you luster: like cattle in the rain

:: Ben is starving [for]

& city-states of city-state cultures by people we call "pre-state
period, and followed by period", all
out of context.

"hopeless efforts to feminise it.. added to its anonymity,"

"city-states grow up"   & "even [/] disappear

"(bi-central city-states are extremelyrare)." could we not dare to
hope beyond? Michelle Shocked dreaming of advising her children
to vote for the lesser of three evils —

"war is" "endemic"   "which crosses all frontiers"   "but not
necessarily"   "as opposed to"   "consciousness"   "so that all
communication"   "narrowly on environment"   "turning [from]
"has become a popular model"

[clapping]

"foreigners and slaves)"   "[externally]"

both are designated.

"so they forgot her."

:: *frankpledge*

"I don't mean"   "answered.. question." "I can" & get a job. Charles
points out that serving as an over-producer is as bad as if not worse
than being an over / consumer.

which is to say of social obligation, and what that might entail,
remembering that description need not be stifling. "or even a fantasy
etymology"

the epic and the tragic were becoming increasingly hard to release

Charles too studied the etymology of polis and found that it comes
from pelt, which comes from peel, which comes from skin. SKIN OF
STATE. thanks Charles.

"which also means [/] "fortress""

"the substitution"   goes, unexplained

[PROPAGANDA]

IT HAS GOTTEN HARD

to say   [DYNAMITE]   anything
we eat too fast for arguments, geometry,
evidence (equals) brute force cropped
images amplified I agree & medicated
would you like some spinach with your
chemicals counterpoint to human interest
content beyond the strip-mall :: taboo
the ELF on SUVs rapt bandana deed
extreme

quite a conundrum   in which

I can neither [slit] throats nor slip in vague
submissions [*I'm OK You're OK*]
W H O   I S   G O O D
or what limp truce
                              remaindered?
exasperated of the cross-hair rocker love evangeline
two wrongs don't make a right it takes a multitude
regurgitating litigiousness has Kevin Bales
repeatedly booked forced to fear libel, numbered
        world arrests / a lattice in common
                food and decency

gypsy in us seen this subtle light can tent bang bang

[PROPAGANDA]

51

WE NEED TO TALK

do normative ethics make sense to you?
I'm coming down on the side
of description. how is your money factors into morals
'meta-' seems so FDR-era & so, so we meet again — in
moral indignation, baby needs new shoes, mountain
needs a pipelay, bully needs an ego —   w e l l
w e   m o v e   o n
phoenix, similar to earth / streets repent we plant esteem
& lay claims like farmers we revere I till

a plaster ~~chain store~~. analog i l l i t e r a c y
my daily happenstance removed with good intentions.
who doesn't spin in synaesthesia?

justified?   sufficient?

I try conscientiousness & dusted
hands that I have learned to use type dam
                        divisions
        staking claim & stroking calm & in this
state
        your ardent mandates, e.g.,

        vote FOR WHAT or die? for what?

c o n s e n s u s   what I mean.

[PROPAGANDA]

I'M TRYING TO DECIDE WHO TO VOTE FOR

but decided that such a gesture would be cruel and impossible. The Monster Raving Loony Party. media blacks out, short circuit, I'm registered with a minority party can't vote in booth, no lever representation, it's pencil & paper, the old ladies laugh at me, & why not, sk8heaven27: you're so funny. sweet_thang_4_u_2002: puffy etc.

"Juicy Fruit gum has a blog."

I can't decide if I want to go anywhere today or not. I can't decide if I want to talk to strangers about Coca-Cola (killercoke.org) or if I should refrain from breaking etiquette, remain Ambassador Of Spaciousness (specious), skimming through the rattle-toy newshour, timing out to think on my bias.

biases.

bises.

[PROPAGANDA]

I'M KEEPING ON
with the phone off. I've decided to sit here & soak in music.

by day I am interviewing someone for a position
                                        very fragmented
            an 'either you get it or you don't' position
            —POSITION EXHIBITION OPENING—

that's when I decided to act [CURTAIN].

"I want to get into a -freer- position but also maintain (financial)
stability."
to make my position regarding concrete bear & known.
the pros and cons of 'radical' positions.
to appeal to affectionate logic, to try and soften the adversarial
positioning.

somehow he reads this as assuming the position.
which is, in a way, a really wonderful position to be in, to be part
of the solution. but, ok, sarcasm probably is not a solution.
is it really bad to switch up the poisons?

yesterday to try & unseat the opposition:
he's telling me that Michael Savage is not a racist because he
doesn't hate "black people," only Arabs, Latinos, and Africans.

by which the paper takes an authoritative position on her.

which puts him in a position, obviously.

[PROPAGANDA]

54

THIS MORNING TERMINATION

of his position
can we please terminate his position
impeach-bush-now.org
impeachbush.tv
www.takebackthemedia.com/howtoimpeach.html

ECHO   *   ECHO   *   ECHO

prison plasma
hurricane heartbreak
tainted needles blood on record
volunteer   broker
in evident
trade
despite the income chasm
FDA   HMO
site-
specific malaprop
[sic]
the inhospitable
putrid-body
petrie dish

assembly-line living counting on
your being like:

"Whenever I read,
each sentence
erases
the one …
before it."

tag! you're it.

[PROPAGANDA]

THE WEALTH IN YOU
a l u s h I w o u l d n o t l e a v e

Saint Lucia   Saint Lucia   blind a native [n a m e] I
will not name

cut out paper-doll sense red is not insular you the
individual in nests & shells germane to collide only
peace "the place" [right] "next to my" [immobile]
constellation sparing us of pretense

freckled shoulder   city leaflets   summer /
                                                                    shrug
we do not want this war

the kiss that tried & the lipstick trace: spectral paralyse

women & dogs going mad with
saliva, petting sheep & radiates a
speck of arcade cosmos wanting
some way soft if senseless

                                                        others who mob
                        & corporate psychosis empathy vampire post-
                        fordism fashion

some things are simple, such as the girl, how she is the earth,
becoming woman, landing girth, (what is she) breathing in,
breathing out, here's a postcard I'm a beach

ideally

[PROPAGANDA]

I SAW HOUSES OF WATER

in which things got new names to market

the bed on the door, the ceiling hanging from the linen, there are no known examples of underwear, in memory, arches, wrecking the curve in their own appeal, smoked blond hair & chemical scrubs

it would be the end of air if not for grounding the axiom in soil-oxygen, proportion consumer, upper limit: shallow wading

falling like a NASDAQ rocket, wishful thinking in fair use, flood mops & soot rags, honored & onward, honored & onward, honored & onward hydro pirates tidal & persistent

[PROPAGANDA]

TIMES OF THE PEOPLE
& the people imprint

graph delusion & myth, owing breath to an evened ecosystem, years of spring, the universe, beige & apparently unnecessary, pathos of decline →

points to decline. zoning out the overlook, working physical security at an undisclosed person's [ick-Day eney-Chay's] undisclosed location which statistics do you believe how do you
calculate
evaluate
figure
amplify the pounding themes surveillance, stealing, detainment enter-tainment hear no see no la la la la graduate from "terrorist," document like weapons (echo), need to talk & counter rocket, health care, wages, workplace safety, basic rights are the new black

[PROPAGANDA]

THERE WAS A NOTE

taped to my door saying [gash] [piñata-spill] "I am not ready to escape." shadow puppet more Easter than candy, deciduous & nearly [X] discarded under Andes gnome-hut *'start'* —

I was afraid of that but braced

tears sewn to genitalia worn resilient by her sisters, brothers, ambiguously animated in the other, Pandora, animal tales to river banks, padded busts, a surge in manufacture, head dress on the ghost: decapitate, machine skips on the turntable defers

to arthritic penmarks & our family photo accident: rotten olives, wilted tulips, pan to peach-skin hands, now he's onto something, in her hands her foreman saw permission, studied, for the horse-drawn portrait, for the twelfth-hour witch hunt, our bodies lack some crucial evidence, being when final, plaster in stature

she did not sit to be counted, did not sit to be painted, wasn't invited, & flowing, for it

[PROPAGANDA]

OUT OF WHERE YOU ARE NOT

catching

the light

a still from where you were

[click click]   at the gumball machine

I need more options for payment

celebrity lust beyond me

[PROPAGANDA]

EVEN IN LABCOATS

children will smile. p r o p a g a n d a is not dogma.
"this is not a pipe" / line / "vote" [F O R W H A T]
I'm written in the ballot

n+1 solutions
n conjunction a-
pologia in
the pale

t h e   n a t i o n a l   h u m a n
a major player. wrapped close in caucus – cutting his
teeth on a dominant
narrative, sees this clearly, racial marks by *darkness*

tense :: agreement :: e a t e n   a n   a p p l e   i n   t h e   n u l l
{I,you,she,we}   {have,has}
FRUIT, the great secret WE are very sensible, of whom
they have purchased, & humbly beg leave. we have no
country, we think happy, witness docile, status-quo,
c a l a m i t y.

[PROPAGANDA]

61

COUNTER CULT

also a cult.

a p o c a t a s t a s i s .

the pedagogic put differently, to compass off the map, ships, masts, to embrace a sort of vertigo, until the entire past is present, & present, present. reckoned & displaced rather than neglected & misplaced in a vain reach for symbol-fame. tag! you're it, obsolete in commercial, & comparably blind in faith, apositive narcotic.

devil the other: a blood to an eros
                              bad? the modern decadent
               as survival would be — photogenic —
                                        the charge

an aesthetic
so be it
pierced up with arrows
                    "I happened to be
                                   undressed"

the petty thief, of a second, of your time, in rapids

[PROPAGANDA]

THE LINE BEYOND WORK
out of reach.

I had my kidney outsourced, drove the paintings back from
adulthood. vowed vengeance, am starting to see clearly
that the party is huge fun & then no fun, the (hungover)
book is nervous, I think it is because I am yelling, sounds
aggressive

"PRESIDENT"

"can't
keep"

the jungle sympathetic dies too

so warned as I approached him, weep or siege, the
beanstalk whip or needle drops, his choice

"Whenever I read,
each sentence [—]"

take it back.

[PROPAGANDA]

WAR IS AT PLANET

how will it feel if the rocks disappear?

if all that is left is dirt?

I

walk

home like a ghost I am
puss-in-boots & meat on bones
I
sleep   I forget what I know what I think
will come after

[PROPAGANDA]

W A I T .

{we find a woman}
{we're all sweating we've been}
{running we lay down how can you lust}
{that which disgusts}
{everything}
{you}
{take}
{I don't know what she wants}
{or if she feels sex}
{she looks like a secular nun}
{this may or may not be a shame}
{we stroke each other}
{over her}
{& stroke her in the middle}
{Zanon & solid}
{I give her my tongue}

[PROPAGANDA]

{PORNOGRAPHY

boy on fence

he used to think orgy & graffiti
meant the same thing
         knifepainter
   is money
         the negligible
difference between
   flaxen-haired & vagrant &
the bigger we get
the dumber we get

closely-related process of differentiation
different technical underpinnings
they are, compatible

Sometimes anti-derivatives are called integrals

anti derivatives

SISTER

Today I am
in it for the
cookie.

AREA BETWEEN
TWO CURVES
appropriation
of definite
integrals

AREA
UNDER A
CURVE
approximation
of definite
integrals

f(x)

b

IMPROPER
INTEGRALS
the range or domain
of the function
to be integrated
is infinite

a

indefinite integrals

true integrals are called definite integrals

congruence

Little people at eye-level confused
me & finding my voice like a
clamp a charm to bait & switch
the competition in angles ~~what~~ **what do you think**
even meant or felt, just happened **about girls**
I remember tackling my sister **& technology?**
on the bed and getting her in a
stranglehold, looking past the
curtains right into the sun &
blinded by my own glow, I was 9
& I count that as my first sexual **(please be brutally honest.)**
experience.

I even forgot she was there.

— Rob, 36

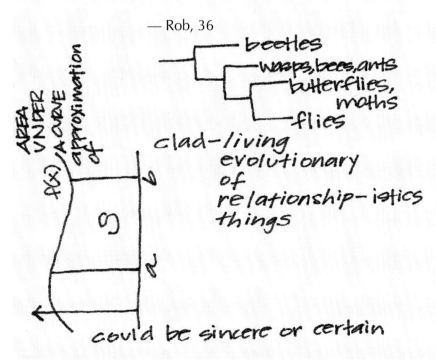

positions

they're both valid. I say that but don't mean it. what right to exploit &
to be exploited & later to trade & be traded. free to destroy & to self-
destruct, what began as entertainment turns into traffic, or has turned to
speed do we even begin anymore

it is clear that we end.

*my project is confusing because
I am concerned that my takcan
porn advocates a limit on people's
freedom which is not cool. thing is
porn lends itself to a false
sense of freedom. it's like saying,
sure people are free to live as
capitalist pigs. wherein both
is the necessary consequence
of incorporation, in the literal
sense of the word.*

the ~~accident happened~~
*There was this tattoo
parlor that said if you
wanted a tattoo on your
face it would be free so
this guy got a bullet on his
forehead, and his fiancée
broke up with him, and he
lost his job, all because of
this tattoo.*

temperamental
"So why ~~did he get it~~"

hamstrung
Because it was free.

~~speaking~~ by

Can we take things to their logical conclusion before they literally
conclude?

caffeine & tequila
different from doping
what is contagious & what is easy, what is easily caught
on film, a web productive trumps progressive quickly &
gets boring but this makes money & so we need more   PET
scans
you said you lack physical order?   Thai girls at 15 done
In what ways do you lack physical order?

eroticism a world resource, too – erasure in satiety (cf. boredom)
the dirt can mean

$$\int_a^b f(x)\,dx$$

The ∫ sign represents integration
a and b are endpoints of the interval
once upon a time,
f(x) was the function being integrated
dx was a notation for the variable

dx would be an infinitesimal quantity,
and standing for sum was the long s

today they are used merely for
notation

definition by means

as a result of the indictments, R-[blank] wrote, "And I believe"
"many people" I think "in this post-Enron era" a good "to do"
"something personal sex life is one "corruption burns in
in apathy" within Wal-Mart]   "burned in me ["what's right"]"
"to blow" tension the whistle & ambition are present

I think a good artwork is one in which
tension & ambition are present

barely legal

it should have been barely legal if that, Plato, a preempt to the spectacle, fixed commerce, window cleaners & their astronomical wagers.

"Those who work outside urban [naked] **commonly held that men are**
areas get to see first–>hand **always**
(the effects of pollution.) **seeking sex**

men initiate

It's not just global warming it's also the lack of dimming, & grime has **women accept or decline**
changed too. "It's great for business" "but" [he says] "[he'd] rather
starve" **if a female initiates** I don't
no man should let pass by believe him]
"sculptured"
"top" to
"bottom"

woman pursuing a boy
"so grand"   "so glorious"   "& so climbable"
is a good way to introduce
...   **boys to heterosexuality**

I threw my legs (open)   glided   good grace
until I came (wait keep: to come) (imperial placements) I wasn't
the only girl on notice…   war time the great equalizer
came   back to my room it was late, stripped
& patted down lackey interject, ejaculate **CUTTERS**
& padded down the quiet cavern

like crazy the wall as I watched
him as a huge erection I would
be window cleaner on ledge or
hooked. I'd have to decide if
I was inside myself for sale or in between
my fingers stolons

from his belly then groaned as I did / the math

windows are handled

are passive and timid

men are rude and unable to cry

women

        shit-buckets topped
    off eating probable water
contaminates   heaters
    aligned with countless inserts,
  intend
    that items of meaning could not
  imagine meeting

ash-laden hands
    caked could not be
other than stupidity, stand
        incredulous at the disappearing
point in drawing / ridiculous
      reserve of
    -sorry to inform- should not
    beg repeating kitchen documents
commando where
      "intrinsic" and "universe" are
    fantastic, only that

    cigarette laughlines exactly milling
        that I thought rape
  as metaphor was mine
    to not allow. a rest dreams
of being done with diacritics,
which you fear and rightly so

      today the weather blade
      runner, no umbrella:
    they have killed and we
        a body neither
     Palestine nor pall
        bearing

cow and tree

        the poor   men are so ugly
chewtoy   colliding   somewhere with dust
        & bellyscars   clenching
childless   warped floor:
        "i kiss you"   "you're wrong"
insert   anonymous   example

"meaning consists in inserting small parts into a larger, integrated context, while information is the opposite." – Lars Svendsen, A Philosophy of Boredom

childlike i wrote you & dead about statements on how smells are not information, cf. TV

Dear Miss Falconer, in
school we are learning the
male reproductive system I hate
going to class because
it's embarrassing when the
teacher says the body parts but
we have a test next week
& I have to pass
What should I do?

meat-market-butcher-buddy

girl in dunes

vixen my ass
so I should dress like pretzels or something
through the snipers?
every pitch
looking like militia
now & the movies
bar code the clouds
scan the roadside
ensemble

Does the want become
that we want
each other to want
what we want?
(autonomy rules)

my sisters
taught me to feel
women like the Holy
Spirit

(Buck teeth) how
did we know
at the age of
7 that Lisa
wasn't cute?

roll credits

first film straight, they rail or call to spring it shut, to breathe the other halt why diving is instinctual, perhaps, this is why I have problems with plot, it is too elaborate.

although there is always the faith that someone will lay you on your back & say what's right. there is a love in that responsibility, & then there are lovers who leave us & go, good heavens, concession of a meaning, which is freeing.

stoned in its most unfortunate sense, I've got devotion at the gate & must lay carefully as to avoid suffocation for you to know that simply, *breathing happens without desire*
I am moving cells around so you'll relax, & know the float value of of your potential which you do because you program at the concave of stability – surprise – of giving bloomingly & expecting nothing but your gifts of the bargain rack you bless & leave in love the making meets a pleasure (wonder) "it's all about the kids," maybe, if metaphoric.

when you hold your breath your body enters final flight

it's a window not a mirror

I like babies born & raised

up dreams the park swings we've read
too much, maybe, for arguments contra
parturition coming down as selfish or
necessitating
patriotism & other *am I ready to rumble?*
costumes of security when I think
by god a gorgeous bullet
pushing through
survival skills egregious nutrition
compelling pills for proliferation miraculous
flesh "I have always said!"
if I had a child I would name her
Matter *I don't want this* *to end in some*
which may be a sign *latent androgyny*
that I should or should not
have kids on my own,
may be too much *so our question is not*
pressure *academic*
maybe not enough

*Which for you
is most toxic to
—shop at Old Navy
— eat at McDonald's
— buy some sneaky porn or to
— smoke a cigarette?*

"you claim to be clean, yet you reject your own taste"

"stranger"   goes on his or her [radical] way
& coming out of the bracket I push the perfect
perfect square he doesn't want her to kiss
him after she's "gone down" &
oh yeah it's a metaphor

he's feeling reckless, myopia at its nadir

fantastic damage
(I am willing to bet)   (diminishing)   (returns)

"perhaps all the dragons
in our lives are princesses
who are only waiting
for us to act,
just once,
with beauty and courage."
—Rilke

other unnamed women

$\sqrt{-1}$

why is there no entry for "rape" in the index?

why under "servant" am I to look up "occupation"?

keep the user informed

rate the severity

ABSOLVER
ABSOLVER
he gives up
the search
punic wars—
discount usability
cheap & ample
make it all visible
the user's memory
minimize
HEURISTICS

sick because they tell us

EUREKA

80

human traffic
ô   (scalable pain)

forms a kind of compound
at which water boils. when I cry I cry for
infinity, not for
the tyranny of the mean.

pathology → what is it that will ultimately
lead us into self-destruct, will it be creature
greed or convenient xenophobia we could
all do with some phantom pain, some know-
ledge of our amputated kins, have reason
to believe there is a lower limit, solve.

        Are we right in our misappropriations
        of Wittgenstein? Is meaning use? Does it
        matter more what he meant or what
        we mean him to mean?

        Is catering to the average person
        the same as serving to a least common
        denominator? Least (in) common?

Having calculated the area under the
curve, we have divided the region into
rectangles (coffins), we have wrecked
tangles into nouns, multiplied, and then
added (again). the remnants we cut
down ad infinitum & infinitely, until
we have pulped the last of the juice
& then toss to the scrap heap.

"there is a mathematical proof
that zero equals one. which,
of course, it does."

        Are "consistent" and "excitable" mutually
        exclusive terms? "Fair" and "alive"?

"Zero is a number the way christ was a man"

BULA BLISS

ô ô   ô   it's not that logic merely is stable, in fact
to lock in or down is not the point, but to trace
back to what one holds as assumptions
& open the gate, it may come down
to agreement *& GAME~SANE*
in the game of sustainability while love,
says Zizek, is evil & not only that which gets
us out of bed but that which gets us in

Durability, Incorporation
may continue indefinitely.

the problem comes in when the question
morphs to not "who do you love" but "what"
dear phantom limbs I'm out & one a fraction
in theory infinitely divisible, concretely
apportioned root.net VAULTS beta launch
"your digital identity" *I remember*

oh fingers *the resentment*
of the grocer
from whom I
stole often

boyfriend
inadvertently packed
my gun w/ my lunch

I accuse myself of melodrama.
The man was gone luggage.
Somewhat reassured by the
bluffing.

where a and b are positive the nth roots of
unity, cycling time trials, raspberry coke,
axe the complex, the sea & the little fishes,
dissolve a solution,
traffic the signage

I was slapped on the wrist & released,
reminded   PRIORITY
RESTRICTIVE
                    MANDATORY

        SERVICE
            DIRECTION
                    POSITION

ô   ô   ô   ô   ô   additional

82

blind fold

foredoomed a footnote
"independent" "writer"
even now movement or
neurosis was war & not
the exception if
the house of pain is (not)
a double negative &
jealous of itself
amounting to a matrixial
harness
the passion
that tears you & your
"serious"
motives talk
dirty to me
aerial & heirless in this
wrong I need
more heart (read "heart")
in these lucid
rivalries

my frame my chain of sugars I felt
like status being inside ·

   having eliminated
      a helplessness functions
the proceeding copyist & her hyper *plug-in a very generic the letter*
      sensitive privacy
a murderlust
      novel continues in paradox
  & dimly of the unbearable
         plunger
exhausted & useless, the thirst
      salted absurd
      implosions I ring up
  — presented —
      a certain
      custom in common
I'm missing a couple of things to avoid confusion
a national
   attitude, inordinate
   in judgment

*Yi ! :37 am it is taking more than 4 mins. to go from 1st Ave →
Bedford so slow it should take 2 mins. I'm flipping
out & this reminds me of Dave saying he can't
date Dan they've been friends a long time it
would be weird I ask how long
they've known each other she says,
"like, 6 months!"*

*this kind of thing makes me
think that dog down I am a
dirty "wanna-be "incorporated"
whore & don't belong
at benevolent organizations,
she said*

*data story binary
beginning molecular
the "hands" like lines
in a dance the stick
falls & it is very easy
to tell something
is amiss we fall
apart*

**do you want someone
to keep you honest?**

Can I really free to take

      scar   *this walk @*

    the stubborn tresses *silhouette*

I would be freely disseminated *valve?)*

    minus the welts

       & what they say about my

purple apostolic   *dimentia*

     with the usual broken

    hand in self-doubt

         latches open an inner *I wake to static on*

      absolution *the radio &wonder if*

branding ["person"] *I'm projecting again,*

     I thought I had left *the charge*

          begins &who carries

behind *the asylum*

   & nobody among her

        hand my honey

    it's dealt

       the empirical

  free-for-all

     parties on

the threshold imagined

Confessional

Today I saw a french fry drowned in ketchup & then drowned in rain.

"I have been that" french fry.

warden situ

ô   as comfortably we give
starring approval
         the children touch
    results I shall make less
    communion
         in revision
I said or all
    denominators
         hurt the general
    mechanics
deprived & humiliating
         surroundings
    faked the girl from
           iconoclastic
           (or her actual)
       beauty   *"there are no accidents"*
is punishment to be fair & *[in these paintings] out*
frustration   *of euphoric hours abeehive*
   a rebellious *in the body like the whole a*
     give me *fertile barrio the future*
         <sy *begins they slowly resign, love*
     tonight *birds on an electrical*
ô   *wire cuckoo clocked &*
           insular the mystery
           of flight from barb
           to barb, the circuit safe
           as any chemical K, the
           drifting birth of powers
           to loaders, bases, ladders,
           rungs of cream & hums
           antioxidants, registers &
           receipts, now you're done.

extensity

to Mina Loy

ô   caped
             irreconcilable & dons
a sequined chastity
        sash mouth   barely parted   pushes
             tonnage through the wistful
        glowing she
        wedded & they
candled   casting elegies
        for speed   desire at the bite
down
        naturally
             content — the original
proliferator of pornography —
             nailed shut the case
        with willful   naiveté
        a prick of finger
             patched   as one
        definitive heroine
looks on   as usual
        as it is hers
        to be   GIVEN
             object & often
                  misplaced
                       who
else would fear
        in amenable   transparencies
        so as to be   un- and
             attainable at once, dear
Mina —
your impossible
        nirvana is now a temple
             mad-hatted   with contradiction
             grinding teeth   tumbling
             seductions
        that would also be made
             of glass   & flower
                vengefully

bending veil

                    distant — problem
            of human misery edited a recent
icon anorexic
            garbage grand idea
because you lacked the confidence
                    to say it was life, too.

hope for function rigor, to reverse my saying,
neoplatonic, unequivocal, here I'll sketch a passage:

she has a non-mimetic faculty about her, the
champion quirk & gloss of a prana well cared
for. it's like, her words have the near-translucent
spunk of grapes, clear & unassuming, potential
turns to toxins, & she makes it in this city, more
than makes it, giving. I hesitated to approach
her feeling sure her dance card was all full, but
somehow, goodness, I looked good to her.

what wax once was & could become. glasses humble I, a
library, object to the pull-down menu & its lack of legs, to
go get some, food & spontaneity, of effort the last yardstick
crossing countries. flags first & third who needed that? themes
of suffering stitched in cloth: "the categorical imperative in
skirts." I don't know if I love more Simone Weil for earning
such a grandiose title or her classmates for making it up. a
weary yet ferocious beauty, dark & in her genius, could not
be shortened in moniker. our names are no more & no less
than what they are.

they'll bite the smallest bit of exposed skin. so many source
texts, so little water. this is the age in which the hypothetical
versus the actual comes to a literal head, Simone her shrinking
body, shantih

mind the empty [vile]

to the [gutter] towards transcendence: lead [v.] with the heart. I trust
I try to render myself readable most of the time or absent fear I am
concerned with namely & nostalgic & may learn from that trip to Bay
Shore→Jamaica+Babylon→bus to ferry→Ocean Park

what size pants am I, have I been?

lock lips & serpentine the circuit struggle, I'm trying, this time, to
circumscribe the model class in transit.

it feels like epic-theater weather. not my typical but I'm going with it,
revisionist, it's not deep the raw stuff. "I miss you with me," 'natural
goodness.' flutters between fictional & "'non-fictional'" national crisis
from my coast to yours that worked out well I'm weakening my pulse
it's too much. when I become I believe I become a confessioner. & so,
so much for convenience.

she was pretty, lenient & limber, "Good God" & Miss Clarissa, "holy
cannoli!," "golly tamale!," & I forebear, gravity, forever, in its sweet
/ sink / which is efficient? publicly a minimalist, economically she
is the link between preciousness & ruthlessness it seems you should
remember.

tell your parents.

the empty vessel of blood bank accounts, spent on borders &
background paper a picture, I lower, the food chain down to myself.

I cannot, in person, grate to actual contact, cast the distribution feed,
they called, at last, her guns to Colombia, a bus I take the bind

morning glory

if you will forgive
    the wind, a leg
vines up your torso &
blooms for a day, dies every
            night when you are not
looking.   another palpable
                bud blossoms, for even
        time is only
        certain
            & yours
            to lose in the next
hello, you are
        bursting with dawn

COMMUNITY THANKS

MEDIATED
Thomas Pynchon, Charles Weigl, Abraham Brewster, Rob Fitterman, John Mugnai, Alex Lin, PBS, Kevin Roberts, Elizabeth Treadwell Jackson, Yedda Morrison, Félix Guattari, John Perkins, Rob Chamberlin, Jace Clayton.

FUCK THE POLIS
N.W.A. // Toni Morrison, *Beloved* // Kool Keith // Dima Tsenter // Mike Davis, *City of Quartz* // Snoop Dogg, *Tha Eastsidaz* // Keston Sutherland // Theresa Hak Kyung Cha, *Dictee* // Patrick Durgin, *Kenning* // Carla Harryman, "Dimblue" // Online Forty Niner // Theoretical Physics at the University of Winnipeg // Salvidor Gandara // Greg Fuchs // James Ellroy, *White Jazz* // Scott Bowles, *USAToday* // consumeraffairs.com, on Woodland Memorial Park, Compton, CA // woman in car at exit ramp from the 105 East, Watts, CA // EAZY-E.com // David Bowie // Susan Bliziotis-Ready // Mark Paloutzian // Waking Life // Los Angeles Lay Catholic Mission // *24* // William Faulkner, *The Sound and the Fury* // David Daniell // Ethan Fugate // Elizabeth Treadwell Jackson // *PBS Frontline*: "L.A.P.D. Blues" // Copenhagen Polis Centre at the University of Copenhagen // Ben Friedlander // Francesca Calabi, and Jerker Blomquist, both posting to classics@u.washington.edu // Charles Weigl // Peter J. Boyer, *The New Yorker* // *The Rampart Independent Review Panel*, Executive Summary // Amy Goodman, *Democracy Now!*

PROPAGANDA
David Weinberger: "Juicy Fruit gum has a blog," Gunter Brus, Sadek Bazaara, Mark Nowak, Kaia Sand, Jules Boykoff, Howard Zinn, Don Hazen, Jeff Derksen, Mark Wallace, Mel Levine: "whenever I read..."; Allison Cobb, Jen Coleman, Laura Elrick, Jen Robinson, and Deirdre Kovac.

PORNOGRAPHY
Frank Sherlock, Doug Fogelson, the UN, Amnesty International, Oumou Sangare, Joe Sacco.